MASTERS OF PHOTOGRAPHY

EUGÈNE ATGET

D1517106

Eugène Atget by Berenice Abbott (The Philadelphia Museum of Art, gift of Carl Zigrosser, Philadelphia, Pennsylvania)

MASTERS OF PHOTOGRAPHY

EUGÈNE ATGET

Text by Gerry Badger

Series Editor: Dr Rosemary Eakins

Macdonald

ACKNOWLEDGMENTS

The author would like to acknowledge his debt to Maria Morris Hambourg and John Szarkowski, and all other recent Atget scholars, for the valuable work they have done in laying low the legend. This book is dedicated to Jane and Emma.

A Macdonald BOOK

© Macdonald & Co (Publishers) Ltd 1985

First published in Great Britain in 1985
by Macdonald & Co (Publishers) Ltd
London & Sydney

A member of BPCC plc

British Library Cataloguing in Publication Data
Badger, Gerry
Eugene Atget.—(Masters of
photography series)
1. Photography, Artistic
2. Photography – France
I. Title   II. Atget, Eugene   III. Series
779'.092'4   TR653

ISBN 0-356-10852-X

Filmset by
Text Filmsetters Ltd

Printed and bound in Great Britain by
Purnell and Sons
(Book Production) Ltd, Paulton, Bristol
A member of BPCC plc

Macdonald & Co (Publishers) Ltd
Maxwell House
74 Worship Street
London EC2A 2EN

Editor: Victoria Funk
Designer: Sarah Jackson
Production: John Moulder

EUGÈNE ATGET
——1856-1927——

Towards the end of the 1880s, a largely unsuccessful French actor, having been relegated to playing third roles in shabby, down-at-heel suburban halls and dingy provincial theatres, was determined to try a new, perhaps less precarious, way of making a living. Accordingly he acquired a camera and began to wrestle with the mechanics of photography, a medium then only forty years old. In the words of a rather more successful actor friend, he began 'to create a collection of all that which both in Paris and its surroundings was artistic and picturesque. An immense subject.'

An immense subject indeed; a subject that was to occupy Eugène Atget — ex-sailor, one-time actor, sometime painter — for some thirty-eight years. During these years Atget lugged a large view camera, a bulky wooden tripod and a case of heavy glass plate-holders around the city of Paris and the heart of the Île de France, exposing a total of 8500 negatives. He struggled on year after year, at times close to poverty, but following his own dictates more than those of his clients. As a result we now regard Atget as one of the heroic figures of photography. And even if his life was not as poverty-stricken or narrow as we once thought, the sheer intensity of his obsession still compels our admiration.

Since his death in 1927, the name Eugène Atget has joined the select few whose work defines the highest levels of photographic excellence. Atget, indeed, stands astride the medium, a strange and elusive compound of simplicity and complexity, naïvety and profundity. He seems to serve as a bridge linking the innocence and adolescence of photography to its maturity. He has been acclaimed a turning-point in photographic history; deemed by some to belong to the nineteenth century, by others to the twentieth, and by a few to both.

Certainly if Paul Strand and Alfred Stieglitz, those dynamic precursors of modern art photography, may be said to mark a radical transition from the Victorian to the contemporary era in terms of a consciously creative use of the camera, Atget may equally be considered a transitional figure from those who did not aspire to be considered artists. Atget's enormous body of work, accumulated assiduously by a supposedly ingenuous, small-time commercial journeyman, compares with that of the greatest photographers of the time. The very abundance of his work — and examples of his genius are spread generously throughout it — speaks for itself. Atget's work may be compared with that of Walker Evans, Paul Strand or Bill Brandt in its continuity, breadth and formal daring, and as an in-depth document of a specific place.

And yet there is a feeling, widely held in the 1930s and 1940s and still residual today, that Atget was merely a naïve street photographer and that he acquired his fair share of fortuitous accidents simply from a prolific amount of shooting. The inference is clear: to a large degree Atget has been made into a great photographer by judicious, sustained and sophisticated editing of his good images — the accidents — by his numerous advocates.

Such a notion gives credence to the Atget legend rather than to the facts. At the very end of his career, a tired old man, Atget was taken up in a halfhearted way by some of the Surrealist circle. Inevitably there was little real communication between the grave, sober, photographer and bright young sophisticates, such as the American painter Man Ray. Thus was born the myth of the garrulous old recluse, the primitive unaware of the implications of his own work. This legend has dogged a full understanding of Atget's genius until recently.

Atget may have been intuitive, but what genius is not? The well-known American photographer

Minor White said 'photographers frequently photograph better than they know'. All photographers will acknowledge the importance of intuition: the act of clicking the shutter can be casual, often half-random – and certainly mysterious.

Atget's photographic method, however, was neither casual nor haphazard. On the contrary, it was organized, ordered and considered. Atget's large view camera, which took 8 x 10-inch glass plates (a size still used by architectural and studio photographers today) required very careful use. A tripod is absolutely necessary, and focussing is affected with care under a black cloth. Slow and cumbersome, the technique is totally unsuited to fast-moving subjects; yet it is ideal for architecture or still-life. Atget's equipment was neither old-fashioned nor naïve, but entirely appropriate to his purpose.

Atget may have been a nonconformist, but he was a professional. He was aware of the tradition within which he was working, and he was aware of his own interests and values. He was also fiercely independent. Once, when asked by Man Ray why he did not like to work on assignment, he replied 'Because other people do not know what to photograph'. A decade of study by Atget scholars has finally shown just how right Atget was to follow his own inclinations, and how his work, far from being the isolated creation of a gifted primitive, was a natural development of a vigorous and refined tradition in French photography. Atget's work marked the culmination of one tradition, and the beginning of another.

Jean Eugène Auguste Atget was born on 12 February, 1857 in Libourne, near Bordeaux. Both of his parents died when he was young, and he was brought up by his maternal grandparents. Atget's formal education was basic: he learned to read and write proper French, and to count; possibly he learned Latin and Greek. As a young man he went to sea in a merchant vessel, but by the autumn of 1878 had moved to Paris where he tried to gain admission to the Conservatoire National de Musique et de Drame, intent upon a career in the theatre.

The following year he was accepted, but mandatory military service interfered with his studies and he was requested to leave the Conservatoire in 1881. Finally he was mustered out of the army in 1882 and was free to pursue a theatrical career, notable only for its mediocrity, with a troupe that toured the Parisian suburbs and the provinces. During this inauspicious period he met the actress Valentine Delafosse Compagnon, who was to become his lifelong companion. Eventually, disenchanted with minor roles in minor houses, and suffering apparently from a throat infection, Atget reluctantly bowed out of the theatre, his first love, and found, almost by accident it would seem, his vocation.

Atget evidently had a predilection for the bohemian life and always had many acquaintances in the theatre and in the arts. According to his friend Calmettes he at first attempted to paint, but after a few tentative efforts turned instead to photography. Many artists of the day used photographs as visual reference material, so Atget could make a living by supplying photographs to painters and thus, in some small way, become part of the artistic community.

Thus Atget's career as a photographer began in a modest way and continued until about 1897, when he changed his emphasis and broadened his ambitions. We do not know how or where he learned the techniques of photography – whether from a friend or from classes, or simply from a technical manual – but his early efforts, not unsurprisingly, varied in their degree of success. Persistence, however, was certainly one of Atget's abiding characteristics, and eventually he built up a large stock of photographs of animals, plants, trees, boats and other landscape elements. The series, entitled *Paysages-Documents (Landscapes-Documents)*, was the only one that spanned his entire career.

The artists' market, however, was a limited one, and Atget seemed always to have baulked at the restrictions of commissioned work, so, toward the end of the 1890s, he developed a new strategy: he began to photograph Paris systematically.

After Georges Haussmann's dramatic modernization of the city that was, after all, the centre of European civilization, there had been widespread interest in Old Paris and in the preservation of remaining areas. Institutions, such as the Bibliothèque Nationale, the Bibliothèque Historique de la Ville de Paris, the Ecole des Beaux Arts and the Musée Carnavalet, acquired drawings, prints, photographs and other documents relating to the

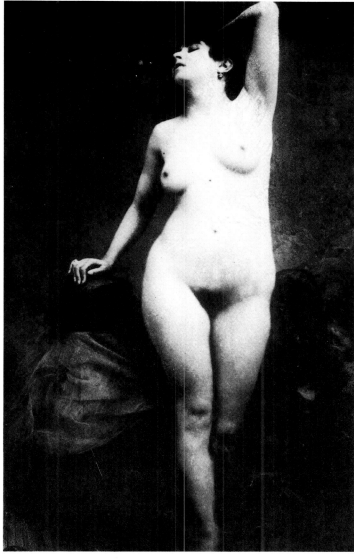

Femme (George Eastman House, Rochester, New York)

guessed, least of all Atget himself, that he was to provide the culmination and climax to this tradition?

Between 1898 and 1914 Atget made and sold the greater part of his life's work. His major buyers were the institutions, but he also sold to many private clients, to those with a professional interest in artistic documents, such as architects, illustrators, designers and decorators, and also to an intriguing group known as the 'amateurs of Old Paris'.

Atget worked hard and methodically. From 1897 to 1901 he made some 1400 pictures of the city and its environs. These pictures were taken, it is worth repeating, one at a time with a large, heavy view camera – a considerable task. Atget's procedure was to choose subjects likely to be of interest to clients, photograph them, make single copies or editions of prints, and take them round to as many prospective buyers as possible. The work required diligence and patience. Much of it – the developing, printing, filing, cataloguing and billing – was routine, requiring discipline rather than inspiration.

Initially Atget concentrated on the more pictur-esque aspects of Old Paris and photographed quais, street-life, monuments and groups of old houses. He soon focussed his attentions, however, on two specific themes: the decorative art and architecture of Old Paris and the traditional street traders known as *petits métiers*, a popular genre of the time. The *petits métiers* represent a unique strand in Atget's work. They derive from the candid pictures of street life he made at the end of the nineteenth century: he gradually developed his images of street people into posed, outdoor portraits of vendors – knife-grinders, lampshade-sellers, musicians and others. When he had collected all the varieties of street traders he could find, Atget stopped photographing people for many years until he photographed gipsies and rag-pickers and then, on a rare assignment for the illustrator André Dignimont, prostitutes.

Atget's early photographs of people, made with equipment hardly suited to the task, were probably less commercially viable than his architectural stu-dies for which he was eminently well equipped. At the beginning of his *Vieux Paris (Old Paris)* series, Atget usually photographed whole façades, but gra-dually moved to more specific architectural and decorative details, such as door-knockers, iron-work, shopfronts and signs. His exploration of Old

subject. Official bodies, such as the Commission des Monuments Historiques or the Commission Municipale du Vieux Paris, commissioned photo-graphic surveys of monuments and paid well for the work. More than a dozen photographers besides Atget became specialists in this field, but none remained so stubbornly independent as he.

All of the Old Paris photographers were heirs to the first great photographic tradition, which began with the birth of photography in the 1850s when some of French photography's most illustrious names – Bayard, Le Gray, Le Secq, Nègres, Baldus and Marville – were employed to document French architecture and monuments. Who could have

Paris moved from the streets to the courtyards, and then into interiors. The *Vieux Paris* series evolved into *L'Art dans Vieux Paris (Art in Old Paris)*.

Although he was systematic and methodical enough in his approach, Atget was somewhat erratic in garnering his catalogue of Old Paris. No doubt he carefully planned his photographic expeditions in advance, but once out in the field he seems to have followed his intuitions. While his working pattern in general showed a logical progression from far to near, from general to specific, from exterior to interior, compared with others in his field he was somewhat haphazard. His viewpoint, for example, was frequently from an angle and always from pavement level, and he did not display the correct elevational frontality employed by other photographers. Atget did not bother with scaffolding, lights, official permissions or the assistants employed by the more representative professional architectural photographers. It would be an exaggeration to say that Atget was unprofessional, casual or disorganized; he was, however, fiercely independent and, to a degree, eccentric.

While never entirely abandoning the general themes of his subject matter, Atget seemed to require the stimulus of new areas to explore and continually re-defined and re-directed the scope of his grand design. Accordingly, while still working on his *Vieux Paris* and *L'art dans Vieux Paris* series, he began to investigate the outskirts of Paris and the Île de France, beginning the *Environs* series as early as 1901. In 1907 he started *Topographie du Vieux Paris (Topography of Old Paris)*, his fifth and last major series, although there were many subseries.

Environs is an especially important part of Atget's work. The suburbs, spatially open rather than tightly organized, presented a keen challenge for the photographer seeking to make visually coherent images. In the royal châteaux to the southwest of Paris — Versailles and Saint-Cloud — Atget obviously felt the challenge, for he returned again and again to photograph the great parks where eighteenth-century rational man sought to impose order upon nature. Here Atget's decorative and sculptural motifs were the carving of the landscape itself. He was forced to learn the difficult lessons of scaling down immense vistas onto the small, 8 x 10-inch ground glass of his camera. This he did supremely well by simplifying his compositions and juxtaposing brilliant white statues against dark, almost abstract masses of foliage. He learned to align near and far objects with precision, echoing the planned perspectives of the designers of the parks. It was at Saint-Cloud in 1906 that he began to exploit the 'faulty' technique of shooting directly into the sun. This was judged faulty because the resultant flare and luminosity tended to reduce detail and consequently documentary value. Nevertheless, the technique often produced a highly expressive and atmospheric image.

Despite tentative beginnings, Atget had built up a solid, if unspectacular, reputation as a professional recorder of Old Paris and the Île de France by 1910. His work sold well, particularly to the institutions. From 1907 to 1912, for example, he commanded large enough fees to be able to sell his *Topographie* series to the Bibliothèque Historique de la Ville de Paris.

This account of Atget's professional activities presents a very different picture of the photographer from that of the poverty-stricken recluse — a hard-working, sober, respectable professional, a trifle idiosyncratic in his methods, perhaps, but not unlike a dozen or so other photographers making a similar living. Exactly what, we might ask, lifts Atget above the norm and makes him regarded with justice as a great — possibly the greatest — photographic artist? To answer that question we must hazard a brief definition of photographic art.

The essence of the best photography might be characterized by a feeling of intensity. This intensity may derive from emotions evoked by the subject matter; it may derive from formal arrangement; it may derive from an apparently peripheral cause, such as the way light falls upon the subject. In the finest photographs these elements can be separated only with difficulty. The best photographers are those who bring a coherent intensity — the intensity we term vision — to their work time and time again. We might also say of a great photographer, as Walker Evans said of Atget, that over his work was thrown 'a poetry which is not the poetry of the street or the poetry of Paris, but the projection of Atget's person.'

To discover something of this 'projection of person', we might look more closely at Atget's eccentricities, for, running like a fine thread through his work, are the personal foibles that make it so singu-

Saint-Cloud (Caisse Nationale des Monuments Historiques et des Sites, Paris)

lar; lifting it, transfiguring it until it becomes not just a record of French culture, but a record of one man's creative interaction with that culture. Atget's images seem so simple – straightforward records of city streets and parks – and yet they touch us personally. We are taken into their world, the world of Atget. We see and feel *his* Paris through *his* eyes.

Atget photographed the same subjects as many others had done before him – even if he did emphasize the common-place – and he treated those subjects in basically the same way as his contemporaries. Empty streets and parks, as well as the more modest picturesque subjects and the more obvious grand monuments, were the staple diet of the topographical photographer. Yet the difference between Atget and his colleagues is striking.

Atget's ambitious, self-ordained project was not the result of simple commercial motivation. In the end his chronicling of Old Paris became an obsession, a labour of love, and from this passion arose the individuality and intensity of his work. He himself wrote proudly of his 'immense production made more for love of Old Paris than for profit.' This love brought him into conflict with the commercial side of his activities, particularly after 1910 when his personal interests became more compelling and threatened the equanimity of his business practice, even though from the beginning he had always made his own judgments about what was, or was not, artistic and picturesque.

In 1912 the conflict came to a head when the Chief Librarian of the Biblithèque Historique de la Ville de Paris refused to accept a survey Atget had made of the Tuilerie Gardens. Angered by the rejection, Atget broke off his exclusive arrangement with the Library and never worked under supervision again. While he did not neglect all commercial work, thereafter it became more personal, more eccentric, formally outrageous and exploratory.

And what, precisely, is the stamp of personality that Atget has thrown over Old Paris? In a word, it might be termed the stamp of experience, the experience of moving around and looking. In Atget's images one senses the photographer's presence. Occasionally he can even be glimpsed as a shadowy reflection in a shop window, hovering over his large, cloth-draped camera. But essentially this presence derives from the fact that Atget almost always photographed from eye-level and frequently at a slight angle, with a wider than normal lens, which serves to impart a visually comfortable perspective to the work.

Atget's use of a wide-angle lens was instrumental in creating the spatial depth so characteristic of his images. He accepted fully the tendency of the lens to foreshorten, thereby rejecting the flatter perspective demanded by conventional photographic representation. But in Atget's photographs this fault becomes a supreme virtue: the sense of space in the picture is expanded rather than flattened; the eyes follow naturally in and around the image. The result is not the distanced, frozen look of a more correct architectural photograph, but an altogether livelier and much more accessible record.

Accessibility is a key part of Atget's greatness. His often asymmetrical, dynamically constructed compositions suggest strongly the continuation of things beyond the picture frame. Our eyes are drawn into and out of the frame as well by frequent glimpses round corners or through doorways. The visual rhythms of streets and pathways seem to flow out and past the viewer, and in much of Atget's work it is difficult to ignore the overwhelming sensation of walking or standing. Almost everywhere the texture of the city floorscape is strikingly evident: paving slabs, staircases, steps, and above all the cobblestones of Old Paris cannot be missed. We feel we would like to walk into and inhabit these pictures, and if we did we would immediately feel at home.

The spaces in Atget's images demand to be inhabited, for usually they are empty. This emptiness, often remarked upon, appears to have been a deli-

Interior (Bibliothèque Nationale, Paris)

berate artistic device. Berenice Abbott, who saved the residue of Atget's estate when he died, links the absence of people in Atget's photographs with his theatrical experiences. Atget's unpeopled views, surmised Abbott, suggest the pregnant pause before the actors assemble and the play begins. The emptiness and stillness, however, may merit a more complex reading that confirms Atget's involvement with the whole urban and cultural experience, not only with the theatre.

Atget photographed the streets, courts, alleyways, parks and buildings of the city as he experienced them, day after day, year after year, until these physical spaces were a familiar and permanent part of his existence. People in these spaces were ephemeral. But spaces and objects — street corners, façades, doorways, statues, courtyards, troughs and gratings — were relatively static. Even familiar figures of the streets were seen by the photographer almost as still lifes.

The word familiar is crucial, relating both to Atget's choice of subject and the way he dealt with it. Much in his work suggests familiar territory, familiar experiences, even familiar faces, perceived and recorded as he lived and moved around the city: the cluttered shop windows into which he could not help but glance; the mysterious doorways and passages through which he could not help but be drawn; the hidden courtyards he stumbled upon; the street characters he encountered briefly; the favoured, magical corners in parks and gardens that he discovered and made his own. Atget's photographs were indeed documents and records of city life, but records of all the small yet significant fragments of visual experience that for Atget conjured up *his* Paris.

As he wandered the streets of Paris in determined search of the artistic and picturesque and simply during the course of his daily life, Atget's mind and eyes were drawn to many things. There was the public face of Paris, of monument and grand design, the immediate bread-and-butter of Atget's commercial practice. And there was the private Paris — the modest, familiar pattern of his life and of his sympathies, although it is unlikely that Atget himself would have drawn distinctions in quite that way.

We are probably most drawn to Atget's personal Paris, for in these photographs we may glimpse a subject observed intimately over a long period by one single, creative intelligence. Atget looked at many humble, neglected aspects of the city and recognized their significance within his own life's experience. To many this experience might have seemed trivial or commonplace (there have been frequent references to his preoccupation with the seamy side of life) but the very act of intuitively fixing those humble perceptions revealed a sometimes serene, sometimes blazing, but always surprising, poetry.

This poetry became most evident after the First World War when Atget turned irrevocably to a totally personal photography. He did not photograph much during the War, and income from his business dropped off. Not until about 1920 did he begin again in earnest, but by then the world had changed and his markets had mostly disappeared. Atget was growing old. He was helped considerably, however, by the sale of a large part of his archive, some 2600 glass-plate negatives, to the Service Photographique des Monuments Historiques. In return he received a handsome sum that freed him for some six years. Atget's work during the last period of his career, by

his own choosing, was unencumbered by the necessity to appeal to a market; he was free to give full rein to his personal preferences. His pictures became more lyrical, more atmospheric, more suggestive and less tangible. Concerned more with feeling than with fact, their subjects tended to become simply light and space rather than material objects.

Now, instead of photographing in the clear light of midday and during the summer months, Atget sought the softer, more fugitive light of early morning and dusk. He photographed earlier and later in the year, in fog, haze and watery sunlight, ignoring difficult conditions and often shooting deliberately into the light to blur the outlines of objects and to produce his expressive flare. Now that he was growing older, he began revisiting old haunts, returning again and again to favourite sites, such as Saint-Cloud, the quais along the river and the Luxembourg Gardens. He became especially drawn to the overgrown and neglected park of Sceaux, on the southern outskirts of Paris, where he produced the last major series of his life.

Much of his later work is elegiac in quality, containing overt references to decay and the reverie of death. It is a perfect old man's art — deeply mature, wistful, contained and unrestrained by the need for any convention. In his last years Atget's vision was set free from the constraints of representation and benefited accordingly. This work is entirely impressionistic, as reflective as other works of art made while awaiting death with equanimity.

In 1926 Atget was dealt a crushing blow when Valentine, his companion for over forty years, died. The loss devastated him. He stopped photographing, his health deteriorated and he died little more than a year later, on 4 August 1927.

And there the story of Eugène Atget might have ended, in a pauper's grave at Bagneaux not far from the park of Sceaux, but for his old friend André Calmettes and two young American apprentices of Man Ray, Berenice Abbott and Julien Levy. Calmettes assumed responsibility for the work Atget left in his studio, dividing it between the Monuments Historiques and the two Americans.

Calmettes' decision regarding the disposal of Atget's estate turned out to be inspired. Abbott, a documentary photographer herself and deeply touched by the value of Atget's work, became a lifelong and devoted champion of his cause. Atget may have died as he had begun, in obscurity and relative poverty, but through the exhaustive advocacy of Ms Abbott the basic lessons of his simple yet profound vision were absorbed. She arranged exhibitions and published his work, which was seen by and influenced a small but important circle of documentary photographers of the 1930s – André Kertesz, Henri Cartier-Bresson, Brassaï, Bill Brandt, Walker Evans – each a major voice in his own right.

Although Atget's reputation at the time of his death was somewhat limited, it was greatest at the highest levels of the medium. It was some twenty years before Atget's own imagery became widely enough known to have any direct impact. His influence upon those photographers who have themselves been influential ensured that the spirit of his work has become integrated with the canons of twentieth-century photography. Today his influence is greater than ever, for our conception of the photographic endeavour and the photographic document has shifted. Photographers have moved towards an emphasis upon the private rather than the public statement, towards a lyrically formal rather than overtly sociological stance. In such a context Atget's mastery becomes even more apparent, his vision even more cogent and relevant. Were it not for the dedication and foresight of Berenice Abbott we undoubtedly would know – from the archives – and honour the name of Eugène Atget as a remarkable photographer of Paris, but we would not know him as a cornerstone of photographic expression.

Eugène Atget will probably remain something of an enigma, for his work can be read in so many ways. It would be quite possible to arrange a dozen Atget exhibitions, each one suggesting a different kind of photographer. A selection of the late parks pictures, for example, would suggest he was an artist of the order of Edward Weston – interested in the formal restructuring of the natural world; a selection of his architectural details would indicate the tradesman concerned only with doing his customer's bidding; yet another would indicate the pure architectural photographer; another the historian.

Yet all of these are facets of one mind, parts of a complex but unified intelligence. Atget's diversity (some would say discontinuity) makes it difficult to fit him into any one photographic category. There is,

however, one unifying factor that shines through his work: his great love for his adopted city.

Atget's lesser works suggest that at times his relation to his subject was less intimate and less inspired than at others. That some of his work was done in the service of commerce rather than self-satisfaction, and that he made many not-so-good as well as good photographs, is obvious. But Atget's profound desire to venture out and record his own experience is paramount. And that experience was a creative one, channelled through the act of looking.

Atget's artistic lesson, like that of any photographer, is an affirmation of the pleasures, and often the pain, of sight. Our fundamental experiences of the world are generally visual, therefore photography is at the core of the arts. Atget was one of the few, infinitely precious photographers who proved this unequivocally. His work, that of one of the purest of photographers, is at the core of the medium.

And what is the knowledge of Atget's pictures? If written in a few words, or stored, as until recently, in dusty, neglected boxes in half-a-dozen institutions, perhaps not much, for we already have knowledge of nineteenth-century Paris from many other sources; but only Atget could conjure up the actual, physical reality.

In the end it is irrelevant whether Atget considered himself an artist or a tradesman. His ambitions were perhaps higher than has been supposed, but it is almost certain that he could not have grasped the full extent of his achievement. His aims were modest, his achievement was immense. He left no written account of himself, only a wonderfully alive statement about the city he loved beyond words and a record of his encounter with existence.

FURTHER READING

Eugene Atget. Aperture: New York, 1980.

Atget's Gardens. Gordon Fraser: London, 1979

Atget, Hans George Puttnies. Catalogue from exhibition at the Rudolf Kicken Gallery, Cologne, 1980.

A Vision of Paris, ed. A.D.T. Rottenberg. Macmillan Publishing, 1963.

FRAMING AND MOUNTING

There are a number of ways to display photographs, depending on your personal taste, the picture itself, your initiative and the amount you wish to spend. The simplest method is to use ready-to-assemble framing kits, which will only take about 10 minutes of your time; but if you want a truly professional look, you might wish to mount or mat your photographs and then have them framed — or do it yourself.

Mounting

Like any kind of print or drawing, a photograph must be secured to a stiff surface before it is framed to keep the picture flat and to keep it from slipping about inside the frame. There are a wide variety of mounting boards available, in many colours and thicknesses, or weights, so it is best to go to an art shop, tell the assistant what you need and look through their stock. Remember, if the photograph is large you will not want the board to be so heavy that when the picture is framed it falls off the wall!

There are three mounting techniques: dry, adhesive and wet. Dry mounting should be left to a professional (most photographic processing firms offer such services) because it requires a special press, but the other two methods can be done easily at home.

Adhesive mounting

You will need a sheet of glass slightly larger than your mount to use as a weight; a soft cloth or rubber roller (4-6 in/10-5 cm) and a wide brush. When choosing the adhesive avoid rubber solutions because they lose their adhesiveness when they dry; spray adhesives (which can be bought in any art shop) are quick and less messy — test the spray on a piece of paper before you begin to gauge its density. Sheets of adhesive are also available but require a perfect eye and steady hand. If you feel confident, they are an easy way to mount a picture. Tape should not be used except as a temporary measure.

First calculate where the picture is to lie on the board and lightly tick the four corners with a pencil or prick them with a pin. Read the manufacturer's instructions on the adhesive and then apply it to the back of your print. Carefully position the print on the front of the mounting board and smooth out any wrinkles with the roller or cloth, working from the centre outwards.

Because the mount will tend to warp as the adhesive dries, the picture must be counter-mounted. Cut a piece of heavy brown craft paper the same size as the mount. Lightly dampen one side of the paper with clean water, apply adhesive to the other side and then secure it to the back of the mounting board. As the paper dries, it will counter-act the drying action of the photograph. Place the picture and mount under the sheet of glass until completely dry.

Wet mounting

Wet mounting is used for creased, torn or very old photographs. Immerse the photograph in clean water and place it face down on a sheet of glass. Using a brush or roller, carefully smooth the surface and apply a thin coat of adhesive to the back of the picture and to the mounting board. Put the picture on the board and gently press out any bubbles. Countermount the board (see above). Check the photograph for any wrinkles or bubbles and smooth out. Let the adhesive dry until it is just moist and place the mounted photograph under the sheet of glass and let dry completely.

Block mounting

This is especially effective for large photographs and means that no frame is needed. Self-adhesive commercial blocks are available in standard sizes but tend to be expensive. To make your own you will need a piece of mounting board about 3/8 in (9 mm) smaller than the print on all sides; cellulose adhesive, a brush, lots of newspaper, a soft cloth or rubber roller, a large piece of card, a sharp craft knife, a cutting mat and piece of fine glasspaper.

Mix enough cellulose adhesive to cover the print and the board (the board will absorb the first few coats, so make a lot). Soak the photograph in clean water for about 20 minutes. Place several layers of newspaper on your work surface and place the mounting board on top. Apply the adhesive to the back of the board in two applications. Remove your print from the water, let any water drip off and place it picture-side down on the work surface and cover the back with adhesive. Then position it carefully on the board, picture-side up. Using the soft cloth or roller, carefully push out any bubbles or wrinkles from the centre outwards. When dry, put the mounted print picture-side down on a piece of clean card (do not use newspaper or paper, which may damage the print). Put some heavy books evenly on top as a weight and let dry thoroughly (this can take up to two days.) When dry, put the board picture-side down on a cutting mat and, using a sharp knife, trim the excess edges of the print to the edges of the mounting board. Smooth the edges of the board (not the print) with glasspaper. Paint the edges of the board or leave neutral.

Matting

A mat can change any photograph into something quite stunning. It will require a certain amount of experimenting to determine what size border around your picture looks best: some photographs are heightened by having a very wide border, others need almost none at all. In all cases, however, it looks best to have the bottom border slightly wider than the other three. As well, there is a vast range of colours of board to choose from, so think these things through before you buy your supplies. Remember that the mat should never overwhelm the picture, but should simply enhance it.

You will need a very sharp craft knife, metal straightedge and steel tape, large or set square, cutting mat and sharp pencil.

First measure the board to make sure that it is square (the right angles at the corners should be exactly 90 degrees) and trim if necessary. The aperture, or opening, for your picture should overlap the print by about ⅛ in (3 mm) all round. You can mark this on the board either in pencil or with pin-pricks at the corners. If marking with pencil, do so on the back of the board and cut from the back as well so that the marks will not show.

Before you begin cutting, it is a good idea to practise using the knife and straightedge, which can be tricky for the uninitiated, especially on the corners. Position the blade of the knife at either a 90-degree (for a vertical edge) or 45-degree (for a bevelled edge) angle to the straightedge. Draw the blade firmly and slowly from corner to corner. Avoid stopping, as this will produce a ragged edge, and be careful not to gather speed and overshoot the corners. When all four sides have been cut, lift the centre out. Use glasspaper to neaten the edges.

The mat can now be secured to the mount with adhesive. To make a permanent bond, coat both the mount and the mat with adhesive, let dry and then press together. For a less permanent bond, apply adhesive to only one surface. Your picture is now ready for framing.

Frameless Frames

Photographs can be displayed most effectively without frames to detract from them. There are many types of frameless frames available in standard sizes, from 8 × 10 in (18 × 24 cm) to 24 × 32 in (50 × 70 cm). Most are easily obtained from art shops – your only decision is the size you need and the amount you wish to spend. If you prefer, you can easily make your own. You will need mounting board, a mat, glass or acrylic, and clips or brackets. There are, again, a wide variety of clips and brackets available. The least obtrusive are known as Swiss clips. Whichever you choose, make sure they will fit the width of the mount, print, mat and glass.

Paris: Place Pigalle (Caisse Nationale des Monuments Historiques et des Sites, Paris)

Avenue des Gobelins (George Eastman House, Rochester, New York)

Port du Louise (Geoge Eastman House, Rochester, New York)

Boulevard de Strasbourg (Courtesy of Jonathan L. Bayer)

Parc de Sceaux (Caisse Nationale des Monuments Historiques et des Sites, Paris)

Versailles: Grand Trianon (The National Gallery of Canada, Ottawa)

Fête de la Villette (George Eastman House, Rochester, New York)

Cabaret au tambour (Caisse Nationale des Monuments Historiques et des Sites, Paris)

Versailles: Parc (Museum of Modern Art, New York)

Grand Trianon, Pavillon de Musique (Museum of Modern Art, New York)

Vielle ferme (Galerie Rudolf Kicken, Cologne)

Versailles: Parc du Château Amphithéatre de Verdun (Caisse Nationale des Monuments Historiques et des Sites, Paris)

Paris: Une cour (Caisse Nationale des Monuments Historiques et des Sites, Paris)

Saint-Cloud (Museum of Modern Art, New York)